Taste Poison
A Zen and Mindfulness Approach To Life

Zen Mister Series
Volume IV

Zen Master Bub-In
Peter Taylor

Contents

Part 2 – Sour Thoughts

Part 3 – Salty Self

Part 4 – Sweet Liberation

Introduction:

Three Poison Stew

Eating poison is a terrible idea. Don't do it. As we strive to live healthy, happy, fulfilling lives, one of our basic survival strategies is not to poison ourselves. In order to do that, we need to know what is poisonous and in what dosages. We also need to know what to do in case of poisoning, where to find antidotes.

From a Buddhist perspective, we have all been poisoned, not by our food or water, but by our mental habits, by how we experience our lives. The Three Poisons, anger, ignorance and desire, simmer together in a mental stew, bubbling up heartache and discontent. There is no way to avoid them because they are part of how we function, how we make sense of the world, and how we react to events. When we take time to examine our lives and seek the source of our suffering, we will notice the influence of these Three Poisons.

The antidote to the Three Poisons can be found in our awareness, which is both a passive receptacle of experience and an active, interactive filter of competing stimuli. We experience all that comes to our attention, but we can work with our attention to examine our beliefs, define and refine our filters, and learn to experience the same world from various perspectives. As we become aware of new ideas, we form new beliefs, which change how we experience the world and how we react to it. By entertaining the idea that anger, desire and ignorance are poisonous, we make ourselves more alert to their existence and we develop antidotes to their poisonous nature. By teaching ourselves to be more aware of their influence, we get a taste of how they affect our thoughts, feelings, relationships, lives and our world.

To taste these poisons, we need to know what we are talking about when we look for these ingredients in our lives. Anger and desire are straightforward words. We know what it means to be angry and we know how it feels to want. To engage with anger and desire as potential poisons, we invite a subtle shift in consciousness. We place them on our awareness radar so that we can see how they function in our lives.

Anger is a reaction to our thoughts about what is happening around us. We all have anger habits, which are how often, how severe, how long it lasts, how we express it, and what inspires it. When we start paying attention to our anger and view it as potentially toxic, we begin to notice how anger feels, where it comes from and where it goes. We begin to notice the anger in others around us, and how it moves between us. As we pay attention to our anger habits, causes, and effects, those habits change.

Desire is even more pervasive than anger. It often leads to anger when we want something we can't have or have something we don't want. When we practice viewing our desires as poisonous and exploring their relationship to our suffering, we find some degree of want or need comes with any experience of suffering. Although it may seem that desires arise without our conscious influence, when we practice building awareness of our desires, we notice that we can release them, as easily as indulging them.

The third poison, ignorance, is not a general ignorance, but a specific ignorance about who and what we are. Ignorance in Buddhism is our sense that we are something separate from everything else. To work with our ignorance we have to practice awareness of how we think about our self. Our self is what wants. It is what angers and it is what suffers. It is what knows, observes, thinks and what is known, observed, and thought. Our self is a mind and a body and an environment for that mind and body. When we approach our ignorance by imagining new ideas of what we are, we make space for completely different perspectives on our experience.

Awareness of the Three Poisons is the first step toward developing an antidote to the poisons. Awareness of suffering and a desire to ease suffering is motivation to develop the antidote. Because anger, desire and ignorance are blended into our experience like ingredients in a stew they each flavor the other and cannot be addressed separately. Because they are part of who we are, we cannot address them through avoidance. We have to engage with them and taste their flavors.

The way to engage with our suffering and the causes of our suffering is with a practice of mindfulness. Mindfulness is practicing a compassionate awareness of the present moment. Now, when thoughts and feelings are happening. Compassion is the process of engaging with suffering with the intention of easing the suffering. When you are working with your own suffering you practice compassion for yourself. When you are working with other people's suffering, you practice compassion for them. Creating an antidote for our painful mental habits is the essence of compassion and the path to a healthy happy, fulfilling life.

On its own, the invitation to taste poison is phenomenally bad advice, but as encouragement to engage with your more difficult emotions and to address your discontent at its source, in your mind, it can change your world. A big part of practicing mindfulness is remembering to do it. Our physical senses of touch, sound, smell, sight, and taste are constant reminders for us to become aware of where and when we are. Every moment is an opportunity to awaken awareness, and if suffering is part of that awareness, to consciously generate compassion in response.

The essays in this book use ideas from Zen Buddhism, mindfulness, and meditation practices to encourage engagement with suffering, to look for its sources in thinking and self, and to find liberation in the process. When we learn to recognize the flavors of the poisons in our lives, we can practice working with them to help us feel better and to benefit all beings.

Part 1

Bitter Suffering

Joy and Suffering

If Buddha said that life is joy, then nobody would have listened to him, because everybody can see that there is so much suffering going on. Buddha drew attention to life's suffering, the cause and the cure, because he could see that, beyond the suffering, life was joyful and he wanted to help those who were suffering.

Life is both suffering and joyful, each in its turn. Each of us is born into this world, destined to experience both. As soon as we begin, we start to feel the suffering. When the suffering subsides, we feel the joy. That goes on and on until we die.

Throughout life, we spend our time trying to limit suffering and create joy. We begin to put values on suffering and joy. If we're feeling joyful, we're winning and if we're suffering, we're losing. If we often feel joyful, we feel good about ourselves and if we often suffer, we feel bad about ourselves. Religions, like Buddhism, develop to help us negotiate that transition from suffering to joyfulness with promises of constant joy. Then, as we practice, we feel like we are succeeding when we are feeling joy and failing when we are suffering. Winning, losing, good, bad, failing, succeeding, all add to the drama of joy and suffering.

There is nothing wrong with wanting to feel joy and not suffer. To limit suffering and find joy, you have to become adept at suffering. You are not bad, losing, or failing if you are suffering, you are only suffering. When you are suffering you need compassion, understanding, kindness, and help. Those things help bring about joy. Some of those things you can provide for yourself. Some of those things others will provide. There is great joy in receiving help when you are suffering. There is great joy in offering help when others are suffering.

If you are feeling joy, wonderful. If you are suffering, too bad. Try not to stain your joy by worrying about suffering and try not to deepen your suffering by wishing you were more joyful. Be patient. Live life. Engage with joy and suffering. Give and accept kindness. You'll surely find the joy you need to manage all the suffering.

Why Be Mindful

Although it sounds pleasant enough, how can paying attention to the present moment help make you feel better? The present moment contains your feelings. If you are feeling bad, you are feeling bad in the present moment. Paying attention to that feeling will give you a sense of separation from the feeling. When you are able to focus on feeling the feeling, you slow down the unconscious thoughts that are feeding the feeling, making room for new thoughts that will help the feeling pass.

It is a normal habit to gravitate toward pleasure and avoid pain. This habit gets in the way of understanding our more painful experiences. When we feel pain we shut down. With a mindfulness practice we challenge ourselves to remain present through all of our experiences and we become familiar with the natural ups and downs of our moods.

Although being mindful will not just turn a sad situation into a delightful one, it will give you the ability to handle a sad situation when one arises. It can also help you relate to others who find themselves in difficult circumstances, because you understand the feelings and they are no longer threatening to you.

Paying attention to the present moment won't always make you feel good, but it will make you feel better.

Good and Bad Moods

Living in the present is fantastic when you are in a good mood. It stinks when you are in a bad mood. That is the nature of suffering. Moods change minute to minute, hour to hour and with each change of circumstance. They change with the weather, with the temperature, with the amount of food in your belly, with your alertness, tiredness, or engagement. If you are in a good mood, life is good. If you are in a bad mood life is still good, it just doesn't feel that way, because you're suffering.

Good moods are great because they allow you to enjoy life. Bad moods are great because they allow you to examine life. When you don't use your bad moods to examine life, then they just become suffering and the only thing that is good about them is that they go away. When you use your bad moods as an opportunity for introspection, you will learn more about the nature of your suffering. This will also help you understand other people's suffering and their moods.

As you learn to engage with your moods and watch the thoughts associated with each mood, you will learn to see where they come from and where they go. When you get used to their comings and goings, they won't seem so ominous and they become easier to let go.

Bad moods are much more tolerable when they don't last too long. Good moods are always tolerable, that's why they're good. You are just as fine in the sun, rain, good or bad mood. It's easier to be you when you're feeling good about it.

So Much Suffering

It's strange that a practice like Buddhism, that is devoted to creating happiness, spends so much time talking about suffering. It is important to talk about suffering, because so many people suffer. Everybody suffers. Suffering is a normal part of life. The practice of becoming happy is learning how to live in the midst of all this suffering.

To be happy in the midst of suffering, you must learn to notice suffering in yourself and others. When you recognize that suffering is an unavoidable part of life, it is not such a big deal when you find yourself suffering. If you think that life should be a limitless, happy, joyous experience, then you will have no capacity to deal with suffering when it happens.

Suffering comes in all forms, physical pain, boredom, fear, anger, discontent, sadness, anxiety, stress, frustration, hangovers, PMS, tiredness, hunger, loneliness and on and on. Naturally, we want to avoid this suffering, but in trying to avoid suffering we forget to acknowledge that it is a significant part of our lives, and we try to ignore our suffering. When we look away from our suffering, we don't get to know it, so we keep on suffering.

When we practice looking at our suffering, talking about suffering and thinking about suffering, we learn about suffering, just like doctors and nurses do. We learn not to ignore that significant part of our lives and we learn that we are completely capable of coexisting with our suffering. By engaging with suffering when we encounter it, we lose our aversion to suffering and we develop compassion. When we are filled with compassion, we can transform suffering and unleash that limitless joy that we always imagined.

That's Just Suffering

It is completely natural to suffer. Everybody suffers. Everybody suffers several times a day. From the instant that you don't feel like getting out of bed in the morning, through the bumps and bruises of the day, to the time you get back in bed and try to get to sleep, there are a million opportunities to suffer. It can be too hot, too cold, too tired, too hungry, too much, too little, too bad. There are injustices, lack of appreciation, rudeness, stupidity, cruelty, all of these things you encounter in your everyday life cause you to suffer. Getting past the suffering is not about finding ways around the suffering, it is about finding joy in living, despite the suffering.

If you think for a moment that there is a way to avoid the suffering, you get caught in the suffering. The only effective way to avoid suffering is to be okay with it. You don't need to be okay with the particular circumstances that are causing your current suffering. You can always take action to change your circumstances. As you practice noticing suffering and changing circumstances, you will change your relationship with your suffering. When you notice yourself suffering, as you will, you will also know the wonder of life, despite all the suffering.

In order to live with suffering, work with your mind, body and circumstances. You currently have the perfect circumstances to learn to transform suffering. Even if your circumstances were more pleasantly perfect, there would still be suffering. That's just suffering. You can handle it.

It's Okay To Suffer

The path to end all suffering starts with suffering. That's why it's okay to suffer. In order to turn suffering into the path to end all suffering, you have to give yourself permission to suffer. You shouldn't look for new ways to suffer, but if you find yourself hurting in one of your usual ways, then accept where you and use it to move along your path.

Besides not seeking suffering for yourself, you should try your best not to create suffering for other people. Everybody is on their own path and everybody will find their own particular ways to hurt without your help. When you find other people suffering, you can try to help alleviate them. That is part of your path to end all suffering.

The way to alleviate your own and others' suffering begins with recognizing suffering and understanding that it is okay, natural and a common experience to suffer. Even if you can't change the conditions that lead to the suffering, but when you notice the feeling, you can practice compassion for yourself or others. Compassion takes the edge off the suffering. When you are truly okay with suffering, it's not suffering anymore. It is sensational.

Suffering and Compassion

Without suffering there is no compassion. Without compassion there is no suffering. It seems like suffering would lead to compassion because one person suffers and another feels compassion for them, but compassion happens faster than that. The instant you feel suffering, you also feel compassion. When you feel compassion, you suffer. They come in a set.

The suffering of compassion is welcome suffering, although it does not exist without the unwelcome suffering that comes with it. Compassion is there to soothe suffering. That moment you feel suffering, that, *why me?*, you think is compassion. If you stub your toe, that hopping up and down and swearing is compassion.

Knowing that compassion comes with suffering can go a long way to ease your suffering. If you focus on the compassion, which is your gut instinct telling you that you don't deserve to suffer, then your ability to see compassion will grow. As your compassion grows, your suffering diminishes. When you consistently practice finding compassion, you will have plenty to share. That compassion will soothe suffering all around you.

Zen of Suffering and Enlightenment

One of the biggest traps of Zen is trying to become enlightened. The hook of enlightenment is enticing. Enlightenment promises the end of suffering. Who wouldn't want to become enlightened and stop suffering? Not only can you stop your own suffering, you can also stop the suffering of all sentient beings. How could it get any better than that? It gets better. In order to end your suffering and the suffering of those around you, all you have to do is recognize what you already are. How could it be any more simple?

That's where it gets tricky. What you are is suffering. Things hurt. Things are annoying. Sometimes things are boring. You get hungry, tired, sick, cranky. One day you are going to die. You get angry. You get sad. You get confused. There are a million ways to suffer. Not only do you suffer, but everybody around you suffers. You routinely complain to each other about all this suffering and empathize and sympathize with each other about the particular brand of suffering that you are enduring at the moment. So how can you end all this suffering just by realizing what you are, if what you are is suffering?

The key is suffering. Enlightenment is suffering without suffering. Of course you suffer. That's why you would like to be enlightened. As you strive for the liberation of enlightenment, you

13

may suffer further each time you suffer because it demonstrates that you are still suffering and therefore not enlightened. However, when you recognize this happening, you are a little bit enlightened and you suffer a little less for seeing that your suffering is your enlightenment.

If you are trying to become enlightened, you should not seek enlightenment. If suffering is enlightenment, you should also not seek suffering. Not seeking suffering is easy, that is our natural habit. Yet we continue to find suffering. If you find yourself suffering, there you are, enlightened.

A Cause of Suffering

No matter how much you try to live a peaceful and meaningful life, there are always people around you who challenge your ability to sustain that peace. Parents, friends, teachers, bosses, partners, strangers, people who care about you, and people who don't seem to care about you, are all struggling to find peace in their own lives. When those around you are having difficulty connecting with peace, they will directly or indirectly, intentionally or accidentally, challenge your peace and cause you to suffer. When the way somebody else behaves causes you to suffer, you can use your awareness of that cause to get through your suffering.

When the cause of your suffering is something you are doing, it seems more possible to change your own behavior. When the cause of your suffering is what other people are doing, all you can change is your reaction. The ability to change your reaction is powerful. By changing your reaction, you can connect with the suffering in you and in others, and you won't be swallowed up by it.

To gain control of your reactions, begin by noticing your reactions. If somebody is making you angry, recognize that you are becoming angry in reaction to what that person is doing. When you recognize that, you can take control. You can question your anger and see that it is one of a range of possible reactions, not the only option. As you practice this, you will learn to use your anger, or other reactive feelings, to look beneath the surface to the suffering that is happening in each person in the situation.

Nobody can make you feel anything. Your feelings are yours. If a tree makes you suffer, you don't blame the tree. If you are suffering, you need some understanding. You have that understanding within you. When you practice meeting suffering with awareness and understanding, you can transform any situation and find the peace you are seeking.

It Hurts Now

Because you are hurting now does not mean that you will always hurt. It does not mean that there is something wrong with you. If you are aware of your pain, then you have the tool that you need to get through it. You have your awareness. Your pain comes mostly from your thoughts. With awareness, you can change your thoughts and change the quality of your pain.

When you feel yourself suffering from a painful situation, notice the thoughts that are swirling around the pain. Focus your awareness on the thoughts and let them go. Now, see how the pain reacts to the loss of thoughts.

Feeling pain hurts, but when you hold your pain in your gentle awareness it offers an incredible opportunity to grow. Pain does not diminish you. It teaches you. When you learn to learn from pain, you see how the pain comes and goes. You see how you can hold onto it and let it pass. It hurts when it comes, but it leaves you feeling fine. Watch it.

Anxious Habits

Anxiety comes and goes. When it comes too often and goes to little, it becomes a problem. When it stays around too long, it makes more problems. It can be very creative. It can be very persuasive. It creates things to worry about and persuades us that these things need our urgent attention. Those things that need our attention will get our attention without the help of anxiety. It can go.

To deal with all the coming and going, it would be helpful if we had only a single door, with a lock, so that when anxiety left, we could just lock the door and be done with it. We have many doors. If we close all the doors, anxiety comes in through the windows. If we close the windows, it comes in through the vents. If we close the vents, we suffocate.

There is no point in trying to close out anxiety, so we need to learn its habits. We need to learn to see where and when it comes and see how and when it leaves. While we're at it, we see what it does when it's there and where it goes when it's gone.

Once we get to know anxiety, we no longer feel the need to lock our doors. We notice when it's there, we notice when it's not. We don't hope for it to leave, we don't worry it will come back. We do what we need to do. We breathe easy.

Anxiety, Fear, and Peace

If you're anxious in your sleep, you may have a dream that you are falling. In dreams you can take nagging anxiety and turn it into fear. We do the same thing when we're awake. We feel that nagging anxiety and we think of a situation to fear. Those situations are the circumstances of our lives. There are billions of circumstances in our lives. There is always one available for us to focus on and make some fear.

If we are having problems thinking of something to fear, people around us or in the media will suggest lots of frightening options. It is nice when we can place our fear on an object in the near future. Then we can feel extra worried about it until it passes and we are relieved of our fear. We get a break. It is nice when we fear something that is within our control. Then we can do something about it. We can study for a test or run from a bear.

Fear always has an object. Anxiety just churns away. Making fear gives anxiety an outlet. Although it can temporarily relieve anxiety, continually making fear reinforces anxiety. When we recognize that anxiety is a part of life, we can see our fears as expressions of our anxiety and objects of our awareness. We can use that awareness to help make peace. We can recognize fear and then confront the underlying anxiety, feel what it feels like, and breathe with it to invite some peace.

If you have a test, study. If you see a bear, run. If you feel fear, be aware of it and make peace. Fears may keep bubbling up out of the depths of anxiety, but as you practice watching the fears emerge, you can see where they come from and make some peace.

Mindfulness, Anxiety, Depression, Addiction and Healing

Mindfulness is a powerful practice for addressing depression, anxiety, and addiction, and inviting healing.

Mindfulness is paying attention to your thoughts, feelings and actions while reserving judgment. With anxiety and depression, the feelings are often frightening and sad. These feelings basically hurt. Addictions of all sorts are ways to find some pleasure despite the pain. Addictive pleasures often lead to more pain, anxiety, depression and other problems.

Mindfulness is most helpful when accompanied by a positive self-image. That can be a matter of faith. To develop faith in yourself, have faith in basic goodness. That is the belief that everybody is basically good despite their struggles. If you can believe that everybody is basically good, then it is not so hard to imagine that you are also basically good. Once you believe that you are basically good, then the painful thoughts and feelings that tell you that you are something worse than good will stand out as wrong. When you believe in your basic goodness and you feel painful feelings, you can recognize those feelings as painful feelings and not mistake them for a reflection of your abilities and worth.

Anxiety, depression and addiction are all related. Anxiety is the constant pressure that keeps you feeling off balance. Depression is the long term experience of negative feelings. Addiction is a generally harmful behavior that feeds the feelings of anxiety and depression. With mindfulness, you pay attention to all of your thoughts, feelings and behaviors. Then you can notice how they feed into each other and lead to joy and suffering. Developing a positive self-image will help the healing process and it will improve your ability to seek and accept help with your healing.

To practice mindfulness with anxiety or addictions, notice the feeling and story of your anxiety whenever it occurs. Notice your addictive behaviors whenever they occur. Do not judge what you observe and don't judge yourself as you remember your basic goodness. Seek help and accept help when you find it. Offer help when you can.

You Don't Have To Like It

One of the liberating secrets of Zen is that even though everything that matters happens in the present moment, you don't always have to like the present moment. If you think that you always have to enjoy the present, you will start kicking yourself every time you are not happy. When you are not happy, you don't need to be kicked. That just makes you less happy.

To find liberation through the present moment, you have to experience whatever is happening in the present moment. Buddha made a living pointing out that the present moment is filled with suffering. Nobody likes suffering. That is why it is called suffering. If you liked it, it would be called enjoyment.

When you live mindfully, cultivating peace in your life, you will continue to find opportunities to suffer. You don't have to paint those moments with pretty thoughts and pretend that because you know that you are one with the universe that nothing can get under your skin. The challenge of mindfulness is to see how it feels to be annoyed, upset, sad, hopeless, angry, bored, or scared. As you practice being mindful through your suffering, you learn to visit with those feelings when they are there, and then escort them right out the door.

Happiness will be there when they are gone. That you will like. Suffering, not so much.

Seriously

Life is serious. Life is also ridiculous. What is serious and what is ridiculous is something quite different from one person to the next. Things that are very serious to some people are absolutely ridiculous to others. The more serious something is to one person, the more ridiculous it is to somebody who doesn't get the seriousness. A good way to figure out what is serious and what is ridiculous is to look at the suffering involved. Suffering is serious.

If you are prone to suffering, you will take things very seriously. When somebody you love is suffering, there is nothing ridiculous about that at all. That is, unless they happen to be suffering because of something ridiculous. If somebody you love is suffering and you find the cause of their suffering to be ridiculous, that is a good time to practice compassion and engage with the seriousness of the situation.

When you are suffering, it may help to look for the ridiculousness of your situation. If you are feeling lonely and unloved while you are surrounded by friends and family trying to console you, there is some ridiculousness to be found within that serious feeling.

It is a serious matter that we suffer so much. It is ridiculous that we suffer so much more than

necessary, which is serious. The necessary suffering is the suffering that shows us the way through suffering. That may sound seriously ridiculous, but it is ridiculously serious.

Rock Solid

Everybody has their own faith in whatever they believe to be reality. We all believe that the world works in a certain way. Most of us understand that we don't really know exactly how that works. Even though we don't know just how it works, we develop faith in what we believe to be true. These imagined truths are the rocks upon which we build our lives. These rocks may be religions, people, books, methods, principles, or even rocks. We can make rocks out of anything. Then we live our lives according to these rocks.

Many of the rocks that we live with were created for us. Our parents, teachers, and cultures lay down all of their rocks for us so we would have something to stand on while we work on creating our own rocks. As we live and learn, we realize that some of the rocks we are standing on are not rocks at all. They are just beliefs. They crumble when we stand on them. That can be unsettling. That can make us nervous. If we find a rock that is not a true rock though, we are fortunate because we can throw it out.

The bigger problem occurs when we find ourselves suffering because of the rocks that support us. If we don't know that the suffering is because of wrong rocks, we will believe that the suffering is because of us. That is a big rock. We go about our lives standing squarely on that rock, suffering, not even thinking to look under our feet.

As soon as we discover a rock that is not a rock, then we can begin to examine the whole pile. We use our suffering to detect faulty rocks. If we continue to suffer, we need to continue to examine those rocks.

With enough examination, we realize that our rocks are not even holding us up. They are holding us down. Then, instead of being afraid of falling down, we become afraid of floating away.

As we break up our rocks we need to have faith that we will float. When we begin to float, we need to have to have faith that floating is fine. Once we are floating we can see everybody around us, suffering and defending their rock piles. We are filled with compassion, because that suffering is our suffering too. We can't just tell them that their rocks aren't there. Their rocks won't allow that, yet.

Dunk Tank

One reason that it is hard to get comfortable in life is that we are living in a dunk tank. We live our lives sitting on a plank above a tank of water, while kid after kid lines up to toss balls at the target that will drop us into the water. Each time a kid hits the target we are surprised. We get an instant to reflect before the plank drops out from under us and we find ourselves soaking wet again. Even though we know we will fall into the water, we get attached to sitting on the plank.

Life is all about change. Change is going from the high, dry plank into the water down below. Change comes constantly and relentlessly. In building a stable life for ourselves, we try to secure our planks and make our targets smaller and smaller, but no matter what we do, the kids keep hitting the target and the plank lets us drop.

If we sit on our board and worry about falling into the water, life is torture. Things will change, we will fall. People will come and go from our lives, we'll gain and lose jobs, we'll go to sleep and wake up, we'll be happy and sad. It's hard to know just what our planks are, until they fall out from under us. We may get upset by the way somebody looks at us or how long a checkout line is. Bang, splash, our plank lets us down again.

Becoming comfortable with the plank, the water and the fall, is the only security there is. The kids throwing the balls are having a blast. Enjoy the carnival. Kersploosh.

Validation

When you struggle for happiness, there is comfort in validation. In order to move from a miserable point in life to a more tolerable place, it helps when others recognize that you are indeed in a miserable place. It is little consolation to know that the world is an amazing place, with flowers, sunshine, hermit crabs and wildebeest, when your little corner of existence feels like a dank cell. Who cares if the splendors of Paris are above you, if you are stuck down in the sewers? Yet when somebody notices just where you are, your sojourn through the sewers becomes slightly less of a slog.

Validation is like the rope that lets you climb out of the pit. You are suffering, your reasons for suffering are completely understandable, you deserve to feel happiness. Although you may not be in a place where you can climb the rope, you could tie it around your waist and know that there is a way to freedom.

The rescue rope of validation meets you where you are and shows the way up with the hope of pulling the floor out from under you. Although your suffering is real, and reasons are reasonable, the hopelessness you feel is a matter of mind. Although the cell and the sewer are real, and you perceive them acutely, you are not really in them. If that rope of hope, with the hook of validation found you, and you believe in the possibility, that there is a way to be happy with who you are, what you are, where you are right now, then you are there. When the floor is pulled from under you, the sky opens up. You can handle your suffering because you are an amazing creature with consciousness. You can move mountains with your mind.

Choose Wisely

There is a popular myth that we can choose to be happy. If that were true, there would be no problems in the world. Everybody, in every circumstance, would choose to be happy and peace and love would prevail. Asking somebody who is depressed to choose to be happy is like asking a drowning person to choose to swim. It is not an available choice.

When you are drowning you don't have the capacity to breathe deeply, relax and let your body float. You're lucky if you can use what air you have in your lungs to scream for help. When you are depressed, you are drowning in time. You are drowning in yourself. You don't have the capacity to access happiness. You do have the ability to work toward happiness. That is what you can choose to do.

When you are depressed your most important job is addressing your mood. That is your full time job, regardless of what other jobs you have. When you choose to work toward happiness, you hire yourself as the only qualified project manager to deal with your emotional state. Then you go to work, day and night, until forever. When you choose to take on this task, you may need to bring in outside help. Friends, family and people in the community can all work with you on the very important task at hand. As project manager, your main job is to be especially kind to yourself and pay attention to your moods. You can see what thoughts are associated with which moods. You can see what time your moods like to come and go. You can see how activity, inactivity, people, sleep, foods, drugs, medications, and the weather interact with your moods. The information you gather will help you and those around you to assist you in your project. It will probably also assist your assistants as they strive to live with their own moods.

Although you can't choose to be happy, when you choose to stick with the task of taking care of yourself and addressing your moods, when you make that choice every day, or every minute, you will discover how to find the pockets of air within time and yourself. Whenever you find the air, breathe deeply. That will fuel your wisdom and allow you to keep making the right choices. When you are more comfortable in time and yourself, you will breathe easily and see happiness all around you. Then you can choose to show others the way. Peace and love will prevail.

Being More Zen

When you suffer, feeling worried, stressed, anxious or depressed, you may wish that you could be more zen. Wishing that you were more zen, is both the most and least zen that you can be. It is the most zen that you can be, because you are aware of your emotional state, aware of your suffering, and experiencing deep faith that there is a way of being zen about things. It is the least zen you can be, because you are actively resisting how things are by wishing that you could be other than you are at the moment. More or less zen is a relative way of thinking about Zen. In absolute Zen, you are always completely Zen, no matter how you think about your experience. Even as you wish you could be more zen, you are as Zen as possible.

It may come as little comfort to know you are completely Zen as you suffer. That knowledge however, may give you the courage you need to stick with your current experience. It may lead you to the idea that you have tremendous peace available to you right where you are. The understanding that you are Zen as you feel not zen at all, reminds you that you have the ability to deal with your current circumstance and any other situation that may come your way.

All the other steps you may take to become more zen do nothing to make you more Zen. You can shave your head, you can bow 108 times every

morning, you can sit for nine years in a cave, and
you won't be a bit more Zen than you are right now.
Those practices may reveal to you all kinds of
shortcuts to experiencing how Zen you are. You
may be less easily carried away by your suffering.
You may develop a deep sense of compassion or an
intimate connection the universe. Even if your Zen
radiates from every pore, flooding the room with
light, you won't be a bit more Zen than you are in
that moment when you notice yourself suffering
and wish you could be a little more zen.

Sunsets and Hurricanes

No matter how much you try to live a peaceful and meaningful life, there are always people around you who challenge your ability to sustain that peace. Parents, friends, teachers, bosses, partners, strangers, people who care about you, and people who don't seem to care about you, are all struggling to find peace in their own lives. When those around you are having difficulty connecting with peace, they will directly or indirectly, intentionally or accidentally, challenge your peace and cause you to suffer. When the way somebody else behaves causes you to suffer, you can use your awareness of that cause to get through your suffering.

When the cause of your suffering is something you are doing, it seems more possible to change your own behavior. When the cause of your suffering is what other people are doing, all you can change is your reaction. The ability to change your reaction is powerful. By changing your reaction, you can connect with the suffering in you and in others, and you won't be swallowed up by it.

To gain control of your reactions, begin by noticing your reactions. If somebody is making you angry, recognize that you are becoming angry in reaction to what that person is doing. When you recognize that, you can take control. You can question your anger and see that it is one of a range of possible reactions, not the only option. As you practice this, you will learn to use your anger, or other reactive feelings, to look beneath the surface to the suffering that is happening in each person in the situation.

Nobody can make you feel anything. Your feelings are yours. If a tree makes you suffer, you don't blame the tree. If you are suffering, you need some understanding. You have that understanding within you. When you practice meeting suffering with awareness and understanding, you can transform any situation and find the peace you are seeking.

Part 2

Sour Thoughts

Understanding Zen

When you get into Zen or Buddhism, you will hear people talk about emptiness, impermanence, ignorance and no-self among countless other descriptions of reality. If you encounter these concepts and they don't make any sense to you, that is fine. If you have never seen a chicken it would be hard to imagine one, even if you've had a chicken nugget. People who talk about Zen have a funny habit of saying it's all right in front of you, in the here and now and in the same breath telling you that there is no self. That is the beauty of Zen, it has no problem with paradox and contradiction. What can you expect from words.

If you hear anybody talking about emptiness, they mean emptiness. It's like when your car runs out of gas and you need to fill up. This need comes from emptiness. Emptiness also happens to be a popular description of the ultimate reality. Usually your mind is full of thoughts, when you stop thinking and experience the world, emptiness is a word that attempts to describe that. If you get hungry, you are experiencing emptiness of the stomach. Have a sandwich.

Impermanence is how things become empty. You drive around and use gas, burn the energy in your belly, the ice and snow break up the road and make pot holes, the winter turns to summer and the ice and snow melt. That is impermanence. It is a nice practice noticing impermanence in the world.

Even the sun will burn out some day. In the 70's and 80's, when I was young, it was fashionable to curl your hair by getting a permanent. This was done every few months. Even permanents weren't permanent.

No-self and ignorance go hand in hand. Ignorance in Buddhism is the idea that you have a self. There is nothing wrong with being ignorant in the Buddhist sense. It is the predominant way of interpreting the world. Of course you have a self. You have a name and you can step through a hula hoop to demonstrate that you are not connected to anything else in the world. We all have a self. We get selfish, self absorbed, and we suffer. When we notice how we are connected to our food and our parents and our friends and our atmosphere to support our lives, we can no longer imagine that we are self contained pods, completely separate from the rest of the world. When we take into account all of the things that make life possible for our self and question where exactly the philosophical line between self and not self is drawn, we can see cracks in our firm idea of what is self. If we change our way of looking at self, we may notice that what we think of as our self, is not exactly us. That's why we can lose a toe or an appendix and still feel like ourselves. Self is an impermanent idea, empty of fixed meaning, so only in our ignorance do we think we know just what we are.

If you ever dispel your ignorance, recognize that you have no-self, and experience the impermanent, empty nature of reality, then good luck finding better words to explain it to everybody else. In the meantime, eat a sandwich then wash your plate.

What and How

A major obstacle to creating the life changes that we need is that we don't know what to do or how to do it. That feeling is enough to make anybody feel lost and despondent. If we find ourselves feeling lost and despondent then we need to make some life changes, but what, and how?

What needs to change is our thinking. To change our thinking, we need to watch our thinking. If we find ourselves feeling lost and despondent, then we immediately know that our thoughts are wrong. Because we have found ourselves, we are not exactly lost. Having found ourselves and uncovered a wrong thought, we have experienced a fundamental change in our thinking. That change can bring some hope, which breaks up the despondence. Change is happening.

As we continue to watch our thinking and notice wrong thoughts creating feelings of loss and despondency, we will also recognize correct thoughts creating feelings of hope and connectedness. These feelings will lead to correct action which will create the other life changes that we want or need.

Once we have experienced the what and how of changing our thinking, finding ourselves, and creating hope, lost and despondent will be lost to us. As our thinking changes, our actions change and our lives change. Watch and grow.

Controlling Moods

In our futile efforts to control the world around us, we use any tool at our disposal. One of those tools is our moods. We don't do this on purpose, but we do it anyway. It starts from our earliest interactions with our parents and is reinforced throughout our lives. When we were small children, we learned to throw temper tantrums to get our way. Our parents would have to deal with our moods and to control us they would respond with their moods. We practiced controlling our parents with our moods and they practiced controlling us with their moods. If we were lucky, our parents had some control of their moods. If we were unlucky, moods would become like the weather and we would just have to take what came.

As we grew, we learned how to have some control over our moods, and we could begin to use our moods to control those around us. If we really wanted somebody to do something, we might become angry. If we wanted comfort we would become sad. Sometimes we knew we were doing this, sometimes not.

Problems occur when we get in the habit of using our moods to control others and we don't believe that we can control our moods. Then our moods, which are at least within our sphere of influence, if not under our control, control us as we try to control those around us. Those around us are also using their moods, consciously or unconsciously to control us.

The remedy for all this mood control is to practice observing how our moods interact with those around us. As we become aware of how we respond to others' moods, we add consciousness to the interaction. That helps control our reactive moods. When we pay attention to how our moods influence those around us, we can see how we use our moods to control others.

We are social beings, so whatever moods we go through will influence the moods of those around us. When we learn to observe moods and see that we can influence those moods, our moods will not control us. When our moods don't control us, other people's moods won't control us either. We will no longer unconsciously fall into moods in attempting to control an out of control world.

Once we gain some mastery of our moods through simple observation, then we can practice using compassion to engage with our moods and the moods of those around us. Addressing our own and others' moods consciously, with love and compassion, takes us to a whole new level.

Negativity Filter

The basic work of mindfulness is to put a filter on your mind. Watch your thoughts and when you notice yourself thinking bad things about yourself, or others, say "judging" and let the thought pass. If you get frustrated with yourself because you find yourself judging a lot, then say, "judging" and the thought will go away.

Watching individual thoughts is a fine filter. Watching your moods is another level of filtering. If you notice that you are in a bad mood, you know to be extra alert to watch for those negative thoughts. You can see if your thoughts cause your moods or your moods cause your thoughts.

When you notice that you are in a bad mood and you see a negative thought, say "judging", and the thought will pass. Maybe the mood will pass too.

Training Wheels

Thinking about Zen is like learning to ride a bike with training wheels. Words and ideas hold you up as you wobble your way along. If you are embarking on a meditation practice, you need those words as encouragement to make yourself just sit there and do nothing. You have to believe that you will get more benefit from doing nothing than you would from doing something. We do that every night when we sleep. We can't help it. Our bodies force us to do nothing for a while every day. To decide to do nothing but sit with some of the waking hours of your day, you need to believe that there is a point to it. That's where the words and philosophy come in. Those are your training wheels.

In riding a bike, when you learn to pedal and find that the bike is stable without the training wheels, then the training wheels get in your way, so you take them off. In Zen, although the words and philosophy will get in your way, it is not so easy to remove them. You will continue to live in a world where words and philosophy are the way of life. You have to be able to live with your training wheels forever.

When you find your stability, you don't have to show everybody what a fantastic cyclist you are by riding without the training wheels. You need to keep riding, always starting from the beginning. To get started, put on your training wheels. Imagine that the universe is not what it appears, then see how it appears. Imagine that it is kind and will somehow support you. Wheeeeeeee.

Speed Bumps

Practicing mindfulness brings a sense of peace to your life because it provides speed bumps to slow down your racing mind. The trick to mindfulness is being kind. We are mostly mindful, all of the time, naturally. Any thought that we notice is an act of mindfulness. Practicing mindfulness is just noticing that we are noticing our thoughts and remembering to be compassionate. When we notice ourselves noticing our thoughts, the thoughts slow down a little bit and become more manageable. When we remember that we are observing thoughts we can also remember to be kind and compassionate.

Like speed bumps in residential neighborhoods compassionately bring awareness to speeding drivers to remind them not to run over children, practicing mindfulness can slow down your thoughts and stop them from hurting you or others.

Without mindfulness, when you feel a sense of unease, worry, anger or sadness, the thoughts that automatically follow one another can run you over. If you are feeling lonely, you may think, *I wish so and so were here, I wish anybody were here, I'm so lonely, who would want to be with me, I don't want to be with me, I'll always be lonely,* and so on until you are truly miserable.

When you practice mindfulness and notice a feeling of sadness, you recognize the feeling and then see what sad thoughts are following. If you are sad because you are lonely, you may see yourself thinking, *I wish so and so were here*, then there is a pause as you notice that thought. In that pause you can take a breath and feel a moment of compassion for yourself for being lonely and a bit of love for the person you are missing. The sad feeling doesn't just evaporate, but it doesn't need to, you can handle it.

Mindfulness is always there for you. Peace is always near at hand when you take some extra time to look for it. When you notice yourself suffering, that is a good time to look for peace. Go slowly, small children at play.

Warning: Words

Please don't read this. These are words, lots of words. They are misleading and confusing. They hang around together, acting like ideas. They enter your head, through your eyes and interact with your constantly changing mind trying to alter how you see the world. They pretend to be true. They are not true. They are words.

Although, these are words and cannot be trusted, these are kind words. When your mind is busy with other words, kind words are a welcome change of pace. They bring some soothing relief to a troubled mind. Engaging words interrupt those thoughts that were buzzing about all the distress in your life. Like putting a fresh bouquet of flowers on the table, kind words can brighten your mind. They evoke feelings of peace and hope, just by showing up in a sentence. They are words though, the peace and hope is something in you, sitting there beneath the stream of words running through your mind.

Words have power. They are like a mental police force defending your idea of the truth. You may be too busy living your truth to notice what your words are doing in your mind or to those around you. They just keep coming, doing their thing. Even as new words bring new ideas to your mind, the old guard is busy defending your truth, picking apart the flawed truth of the new words. Of course the new words are carrying a flawed truth. They are words.

These words are written for people who are being held hostage by their own words. They are arranged to highlight the importance of kindness, peace and hope, which is not contained in words, but beyond them. When you have recognized the source of peace in your life, your words will reflect that and there will be silence.

Words and Worries

It takes a thief to catch a thief. It is the same with words and worries. Worries are based in words. Thoughts are built on words. Before you had words, you had only experiences. You did not worry what the next experience would bring. You did not worry about what had happened to you. Your preverbal life was lived fully in the present. Then words came along.

Once you developed language, then you had a framework for your thoughts. That framework makes you able to function in life. It also creates a lot of anxiety. When you are able to string thoughts together you can look reflectively into the past and speculatively into the future. Either way you look, you see your Self blink into or out of existence. That causes a lot of worry. Most worries are not about being and not being. They are more about being or not being good enough, capable enough, worthy enough, likable enough, right enough and those worries extend beyond you to those around you. These worries are all made up of stories that you were told and tell yourself. Those stories are all told in words.

The simple thing to do is to stop the words. Stop thinking. Worries will vanish. However, the first thing that happens when you try to stop thinking is that you start to think. You think a word or two. In order to work your way out of worries, you need some words to talk you down. The words that you are good enough, capable enough, worthy enough, likable enough are not enough. You have to be able to experience that for yourself. Words can tell you that you have a higher Self that is beyond all that worry. You can experience that Self by sitting still and minding the present moment. How would you ever know that if words weren't there to point the way?

To experience that Self for yourself, you have to notice your worries, see the stories of the worries, and watch the words. When the words are making worries, make them stop. No words, no worries. Word.

Watch Your Words

Words are the breadcrumb trail we leave behind us to find our way home. We rely on them, but, like Hansel and Gretel discovered, they don't get you home. When you are looking for the Truth, you have to go beyond words. You have to learn the territory, so that you know your way home, with or without the breadcrumbs.

You cannot live without words. After you learn language, they are how you think. All day long, words, words, words. The words are cagey and run through your head acting just like the voice of God telling you how things are. They make positive statements like *it is hot, that is sad, this is impossible, that is good, this stinks.* The words just keep coming telling you how things are. They can lead you deep into the forest and leave you there, where witches dwell.

In order to find your way home, you only need to pay attention to the words running through your mind. You can see the path where you drop the crumbs. This crumb is next to a stone, that one is near a mossy stump, then you will know how to get home after the birds have cleared your trail. The Truth is right next to the words, even if the words are completely wrong.

If the words that habitually blaze trails in your mind have left you in the forest, you can always find your bearings by shutting them down.

You can breathe in a big lungful of air, look into the sky, hug your friend and not let any words distract you from your experience. Words will swirl around each experience, *the sky is blue, this breath feels good, my friend is amazing*, but you are watching them so they don't lead you away from the moment. You are home.

A Bit of Truth

There is the Truth, and there is talking about the truth. The history of the world is a story. The life of Buddha, the life of Jesus, and the life of Mohamed are all stories about people who tried to interpret the Truth. Once an experience is written down it is a story, it is not the Truth. If you want to convey how an apple tastes, you can talk about flavor, texture, good or bad, but only you know how that apple tasted to you. That experience is lost on the rest of us. We can experience your words but we will forever wonder just how that apple tasted.

If you want to know the Truth, live your life. That is your truth. Your thoughts, feelings and sensations are little bits of the Truth speaking to you. Listen. Watch. Wonder.

Look Again

Everything can be fine if you can look at it from a new perspective. Finding that new perspective is the challenge. To find a new perspective, first you need to throw out your current perspective. Throwing out your perspective does not mean ignoring what you observe in your circumstances, it only means changing how you react to the facts. If you stub your toe on a rock, then your toe will hurt. If your perspective uses the fact of your hurt toe to confirm that you are clumsy, or to become angry because somebody put a rock where a rock shouldn't be, then your perspective is causing you additional pain and making the situation worse. When you notice that happening, you need to throw out that perspective and look again.

In order to throw out the perspective, it helps to recognize that the perspective is wrong. If you feel excessive anguish, worry, anger, fear, or anxiety then you can assume that your perspective is wrong. You are looking at things in a way that makes them seem less than fine. If you know that above or beneath it all things are fine, then you can ask yourself, *how is this fine*? An answer will always come to you.

Recognizing that things are fine, does not mean that you always have to be happy about how they are. You can be sad and fine, angry and fine, scared and fine, or worried and fine. You can even be terminally ill and fine from a certain perspective. If you cannot see that things are fine, or imagine that they could be fine, then you need to take a breath, clear your mind and look again. You'll be fine.

Buffalo Wings

Like hot buffalo wings, anxious moments come in 99 different varieties. They range from honey mustard, to hell fire, to suicide. One of the pleasures of eating buffalo wings comes from pushing your spicy comfort zone. There is no such pleasure in the anxious moments, but every variety of pain that they produce can be managed with awareness. If you dig into your anxiety like a plate of hot wings, before long, it will be gone and you will be left snacking on celery and carrot sticks.

The trick to eating hot wings is to look for the flavor beyond the burning heat of the hot sauce. In dealing with anxiety, the flavor is in the thoughts. Observe how the thoughts and anxiety arise together, creating and feeding each other. If you think that the thoughts cause the anxiety, then the thoughts gain credibility and the anxiety will feed on those thoughts, turning an order of mild wings into a five alarm special. If you believe that the anxiety causes the thoughts, then you will not be carried away by the imagined doom that your thoughts predict. The moment you recognize your anxiety, you can engage your awareness. As you feel the burn of the anxiety, you understand that the thoughts are reactionary and unreliable.

If you take only one bite of a super hot wing, the burn will remain in your mouth even as you guzzle water. With anxiety too, you can drink water to help the heat of the moment pass. It's still not instantaneous relief, but it helps. Although the thoughts may not cause the anxiety, they can help it pass. Consciously take a deep breath, a drink of water and, thought by thought, refute and release the wrong thoughts of anxiety.

As you focus your attention on the feeling of anxiety, recognizing the varieties and flavors, you gain a sense of control. When an anxious feeling occurs, watch the accompanying thoughts pass like a winged buffalo.

Whenever you are served a plate of anxiety, sample the feeling, determine the variety, see the thoughts, take a breath, or a drink of water, and engage your awareness. The anxiety will pass, and you will be well, snacking on carrots and celery.

Faith In Delusion

If you had the same kind of faith in your delusion as you have in your reality, your reality would not seem so daunting. Developing faith in delusion is a practice in paradox. The more deluded you believe yourself to be, the less able you are to believe yourself at all. The less deluded you believe yourself to be, the more rigid your reality seems. When your reality seems overwhelming, exploring your delusion may give you some flexibility.

Despite our delusions, reality is real. The question remains about what that is and what we should do with it. When we don't question reality, we just assume that reality is what it seems to be. At one level, reality is exactly what it seems to be. At another level, reality is not at all what it seems to be. Having faith in your delusion is believing that both these levels exit together.

The mediating force between the real and perceived real is you, your experiences and your beliefs. You have the knowledge of the world at your disposal to help you decide what to believe or not. You have friends, family, doctors, monks, clerics, sages, clowns, scientists, poets, artists, who are there to help you negotiate your reality. You also have your senses and your feelings. As all of these guides work with you to help you define reality, reality is changing. What was true in 2500

63

years ago is not true today. What is true in India, is not true in Indiana. Yet all you have to work with is your best guess at what is real and true where and when you are. The error in your guess is your delusion.

You can be comfortable with reality and in harmony with reality without understanding or even approving of reality. Your mind makes your reality and it can change it. With all the unknowns, misinterpretations, misrepresentations, and complexities of the world, it is necessary to become comfortable with not knowing. Although you can't know what you don't know, you can have faith that you don't know all that you know. What you think is good, may be bad and bad may be good. That's why good and bad are overrated. Have faith in your ability, in your knowledge, and in your delusion. You never know…

True to You

Whatever you believe will determine how you experience life. How you determine what is true to you is largely based on who you trust. The most important person to trust is yourself. You are certainly not the only person who you can trust, but you are the most important. If you can't trust yourself, you cannot trust your ability to trust anybody. You actually have no choice but to trust yourself. Even if you didn't trust yourself, you would still influence yourself as you acquire and discard beliefs. You either believe or you don't. You must trust yourself in order to figure out what is true to you.

What is true to you continually changes. The more you practice trusting yourself to find the truth, the easier it is to discard false beliefs and acquire more true beliefs. If you place too much trust in your beliefs, or in other people's beliefs, then you will try to hold on to those beliefs even when you begin to suspect that they might be wrong. When you trust yourself more than your beliefs, then you are flexible in taking on and shaking off beliefs. Eventually, as you remain true to you, your beliefs will be flexible and you will be confident in them and yourself.

When you remain true to you, you can trust easily and well. Even if others betray your trust, you can remain unshaken with your truth intact. It's your truth. Wear it wisely.

Comfortable Thoughts

If you are uncomfortable, you are not comfortable with your thoughts. To become comfortable, you have to change your thoughts. Changing your thoughts is not the difficult part. Thoughts change all the time. When you are uncomfortable, your thoughts are going from one uncomfortable place to the next. When this happens, it's time for some new thoughts. The first step in finding a new set of thoughts is seeing what thoughts you already have. Looking at your uncomfortable thoughts with the hope of transforming them is already a change. When you do that, the transformation has begun.

The most comfortable thought there is, *everything is going to be all right*. That thought is a good thought to turn to when the opposite seems true. Another comfortable thought is, *everything is all right*. That's what parents say to kids when they are in distress. *It's ok. It's ok.* That can be a comfortable thought. A more testable thought is, *everything has been all right.* The thoughts, *everything is* and *will be all right,* tend to contradict the immediate experience of discomfort. With the thought, *everything has been all right*, you can look back over your life and see all the events you have survived and all the events your ancestors endured to get you to the present moment. You can see that despite so many horrific events, you have come to a moment of hope, where you are focused on becoming comfortable with your thoughts.

When you understand or believe that everything is, was and will be all right, then uncomfortable thoughts are not so uncomfortable. Circumstances will continue to test your ability to be comfortable with your thoughts. Whenever discomfort creeps into your thoughts, observe the discomfort, observe the thought. If there is a pebble in your shoe, throw it out. If your mind is pestering you, throw it out. When you look up into the sky, your thought is the sky. It's wide open, with lots of room for thoughts. As a bird flies by, it doesn't leave a trace in the sky. When you give your thoughts that kind of space, the thoughts pass. Everything is ok, comfortable.

No Thoughts

Just beneath deep thoughts are no thoughts. No thoughts are also above and below shallow thoughts. Deep thoughts, shallow thoughts, and no thoughts are part of life. Thoughts are wildly entertaining. They can lead to wonderful achievements and cause all kinds of distress. Some thoughts are peaceful. No thoughts are peaceful. Great thinkers are also great non-thinkers. Don't think about that. How peaceful.

Part 3

Salty Self

Who Are You?

To be at peace, it is essential to know who you are, because you are who you are. You have always been you and you will never be anything but you. Nothing you do or think will change who you are. What you do and think though, can make you more at peace with yourself.

If you are not at peace with yourself, then you are missing who you are. You are likely thinking of characteristics, skills or possessions that you lack and would like to have, or have and would like to lack. You may be imagining relationships you would like to have, or relationships that you have but wish you didn't. Those things are not who you are. Those are all circumstances.

Who you are is much more fundamental than what you do, what you have, or the people around you. Who you are is beyond any characteristics or credentials that you associate with yourself. When you know who you are, you will be at peace with yourself. It is possible to be at peace with yourself regardless of your circumstances. When you know your essence, you will know peace.

Understanding Ego

The difference between you and your ego is your ego doesn't bleed. Your ego doesn't know that it doesn't bleed. If you cut your finger, your ego thinks, *oh no, I'm bleeding.* That is how closely your ego identifies itself with you. How closely you identify with your ego determines the quality of your suffering.

When you develop an understanding of ego, you can also gain some understanding for ego. To develop this understanding, go on an ego watch. Your ego is always with you, so it is always available to see. It pretends that it is you, so one way to spot your ego is to look in the mirror. When you see yourself in the mirror that is just your image. Your ego will show itself by offering opinions about the image, good or bad. If you are watching for ego, you can acknowledge those opinions and let them pass. If you are not watching for ego those opinions will settle into the core of your being and be added to a long list of unexamined truths about yourself. That list, quietly, subversively compiled by your ego, determines how you suffer.

In understanding ego, it is not helpful to vilify your ego. Although your ego actively contributes to your suffering, it is also your ego that suffers for you. If you see your ego as an evil entity, you will experience a great sense of justice, because your ego is constantly and immediately punished by each bit of suffering it creates in you. Unfortunately, you cannot enjoy that sense of justice, because as your ego suffers, you suffer. When you see that your ego is suffering for you and as you, then you find some compassion for your ego. Noticing how your ego suffers is part of watching for ego. If you notice yourself suffering, you can look into that suffering and see your ego.

You can also watch for your ego in your pride. If you notice yourself seeking confirmation for your worth in external circumstances, that is your ego building its house of cards. As circumstances change and the cards fall, your imagined worth will be gone. Your worth will still be there, but your ego's definition of your worth will be lost and it will suffer, so you will suffer. You are totally worthy, but you suffer from lack of worth.

When you become adept at observing your ego, you will understand that you are both separate and inseparable from your ego. You can observe your ego through your thoughts, opinions, judgments, feelings, pride, shame, suffering, and joy. When you understand your ego, you can't help but admire and appreciate it, because it is going through the trenches for you. If you begin to bleed, your ego will help get you a band-aid. It too has compassion.

Beautiful Mirror

You don't have to look in the mirror to see that you're beautiful. It is probably easier to see your beauty by not looking in the mirror. When you look in the mirror at yourself, you tend to see your ego. You see your features and you have all kinds of ideas about this or that feature. Even though you are filled with beauty, you may look at a mirror and miss it entirely. To see beauty, you have to be a beautiful mirror.

Being a beautiful mirror is simple. All you have to do is recognize beauty. If you see a flower and think that it's beautiful, you are a beautiful mirror. If you taste a delicious bit of food, you are a beautiful taste mirror. If you enjoy hearing a song, you are a beautiful sound mirror. The world is full of beauty to reflect. The beauty is not in the flower, food, or music. It is in you. Without you, the flower is just a flower, trying to be beautiful to a bee. The bee may see beauty too, but that beauty is in the bee.

As a mirror, you also reflect the ugliness of the world. That's what mirrors do, they reflect. Because you reflect ugliness, that does not make you ugly, it makes you a beautiful mirror, reflecting what you encounter, beautifully.

Measuring Yourself

There are many ways to measure yourself. You can measure yourself in feet, inches, meters, centimeters, pounds, kilograms, stones, degrees Fahrenheit, Celsius, years, months, IQ, EQ, dollars, cents, Euros, shillings, grades, degrees, personality, friends, happiness, suffering, and so on and so on. All these ways of measuring yourself represent ideas about yourself. Each form of measurement though, is as imaginary as your self.

They are all real ideas, just like the idea of your self is real. Measurements break things down and provide new perspectives on how to look at things. A tree is the height of a tree regardless of meters and inches. We can take the tree and cut it up into 2x4s and we have all kinds of measurements, but no more tree. A year of our lives has so many days and nights and events. Those events go on regardless of how we divide the time.

The idea of a separate self is just another idea of measurement. Instead of one entire universe, there is a universe made up of so many parts and we count ourselves as one of those parts, separate from the whole. For some reason, that basic measurement, making two out of one adds to our experience of suffering. It's unfathomable.

Self Positive

As long as you experience a self, you should feel good about yourself. A good feeling about yourself is the best lie detector you can apply to your thoughts. If your thoughts are thinking things about you that make you feel bad about yourself, then those thoughts are simply wrong. They should not be ignored. They should be actively thrown out.

If you want to criticize yourself, you can criticize your behavior. That is not exactly you, and that you can change though compassionate criticism. If your criticism of your behavior digresses into criticism of your self, then you can use your knowledge of your positive self to recognize those destructive thoughts and toss them away. With behavior, if you notice you have behaved in a way that has hurt somebody, you can apologize. Critically observing your behavior while, believing in your positive self prevents you from critically wounding yourself. Making choices with the guidance of your positive self gives you the benefit of your own wisdom.

If you don't understand that you are fundamentally wonderful, you may not notice that your negative thoughts about yourself are wrong. If that is your condition, listen, those thoughts are wrong. You may owe yourself an apology. You deserve good feelings. You should get to know your positive self.

Greatness

It's time to recognize your greatness. Your potential for greatness doesn't matter, that has nothing to do with anything. Your greatness cannot be compared to anybody else's greatness, because that is their greatness. Your greatness cannot be measured by your attitude or accomplishments. Your greatness sits in your heart of hearts and expresses itself though everything that you do. Even doubting your greatness is an expression of your greatness.

Recognizing greatness in others is also part of your greatness. It doesn't matter if others can see your greatness or not. If they can't, that is their limitation, as they do not understand their own greatness. They likely believe that there is a limited amount of greatness in the world and they are trying to compete for scraps. When you recognize your greatness, you cannot hide it. It shines through everything you do.

Once your recognize your greatness, life gets a little easier because you no longer have to compete. You are free to be you. If you hurt, you don't hurt because you are not great. You hurt because you hurt. If you choose to compete, your style is marked with kindness and compassion and the prize is not demonstrating your greatness, but helping others to recognize theirs. Mighty great of you.

Delusions – Self and Other

If you want to imagine how delusion works, just look at everybody around you. You can imagine that you are not deluded and that you understand the Truth. Then, as you interact with the world, see how you are able to recognize how other people seem to get it wrong. They may wear clothing that is out of fashion. They may say things that make you cringe. They may be sad about something that you know is unimportant. They may think that they are ugly when they are beautiful. They may think they know things that they don't. They may do things to hurt themselves or others, even on purpose. Because you know the truth, you can see how others' way of seeing the world causes them to do these things. Delusion is everywhere.

Once you get comfortable with seeing everybody else's delusions, then you can begin to see your own. You can begin by looking at an earlier incarnation of yourself. You can look back to an earlier point in your life when you thought you knew things. Now, you may know better, or at least differently. It's hard to see all that delusion around you and in you and not imagine that some is still happening.

Once you embrace the possibility of delusion in yourself and everybody around you, you are free to question everything. If something seems terrible, it may not be. If something seems wonderful, it well could be. Terrible and wonderful get all mixed up. When you see somebody else feeling terrible because of their particular delusion, you will be able to feel compassion for them, because you know a little something about how delusions work. When you feel terrible, because of your delusion, you can feel compassion for yourself. We are all small children in a big world, just trying to figure things out. It seems wise to act with kindness and compassion, at least until we know better.

Reality Check

Reality is slippery. There are the laws of the land, the laws of language, the laws of physics, the laws of the universe, and then there is Reality. You shouldn't need a lawyer to check in with reality. You interpret reality with your mind. Your mind is full of creative powers and whatever you consider to be reality was created by your mind. In interpreting the laws of the universe, the laws of nature, the rules of your house and the social etiquette of all the circles you travel in, your particular reality is born. That reality, because it is your mind's interpretation and creation, is also your delusion. To happily coexist with your delusions, it is a good practice to check in with reality and check out what reality is.

Checking reality is checking your mind. That's all you can do. Your mind checks in with you with feelings and ideas. Reality is how you feel. Reality is what you see and hear. Reality is the thoughts that pass through your head. Reality is the air you breathe. Reality is the taste of your food. Reality may be that you are one with the universe. Reality may be that you are a luminous being. That is why you need to check reality. Anything is possible.

Reality is constantly changing. Your delusions are constantly changing. Your mind is constantly changing. Check it out.

Perspective

You live your life from your perspective. It can't be any other way. Over time, you change and your perspective changes. How you see things when you were three years old is different from how it is now. Your perspective changes slightly with each new experience. Some experiences will cause big shifts, while others are imperceptible. Every time your mood changes, your perspective changes. It changes with the hours of the day. It changes as you move from place to place. This constant change is your window to the world. When you feel like you are stuck in a situation, that is one perspective. Because it is your perspective, it is the only one available, but it can change and it will change.

Life gets lonely when lived from one perspective. That is why everybody is constantly sharing their opinions and observations with each other. If things seems lousy, talk to a person with a different perspective. If they are able to help you, you may feel you have gained some perspective. You haven't gained anything. You have experienced another change.

Your perspective is incredibly versatile. You can imagine life as the universe or as a bug. Both the universe and bugs have generally peaceful perspectives, which is why it's nice to practice seeing life from those other angles. There is always a peaceful point of view available to you. As you experience life's changes, practicing awareness of the peace available in the present moment makes it easer to live with all the unsettling influences. If you think you have problems, that is one perspective, but it can change. Look again. Adjust your focus. Notice where the peace is. When you can see peace, you have a great perspective.

Beside Yourself

When people feel strong emotions, they may describe themselves as being beside themselves. People can be beside themselves in love or in hate. Strong emotions do that. The heat of the feeling can be so intense that your psyche has to step away from the flame and you may find yourself beside yourself.

There are other circumstances, sometimes in near death or traumatic experiences, sometimes in deep meditation, where people have out of body experiences. People report that they are able to observe themselves from a vantage point, which may include a view of the back of their own head.

Even more common, is the feeling of hating yourself, or not being able to live with yourself. The antidote to this situation, or to feelings of low self esteem in general, is often thought to be to learn to love yourself. Whether you are loving yourself, hating yourself, or floating above or beside yourself, you are having a unique experience of yourself. Becoming two selves, subject and object self, raises the question of what the heck are you?

If you think that you hate yourself, what is it that hates? What is hated? What is hate? That subjective self that hates the objective self can't really be paying attention. People naturally love themselves. That is why we gravitate toward pleasure and try to avoid pain. We are always looking for ways to be happy. Hating ourselves is a sign of frustration that we are not able to provide adequate happiness for ourselves, or those around us are not helping us to find the happiness we deserve. Loving ourselves is what we are doing beneath hating ourselves, but either way we are beside ourselves.

Loving yourself is not necessarily the antidote to hating yourself, it is what's left when you stop hating yourself. Recognizing that you are hating yourself and examining what it is that you are thinking of as yourself is the beginning of coming to terms with the hate.

If you notice yourself hating yourself, then you can recognize that you are beside yourself and in a perfect position to help. Is that part that hates any better than the hated? Which part is suffering more? What is your deepest wish? Is it to increase your suffering or increase your happiness? If you struggle with these questions long enough, you may find yourself as one, two, ten thousand, or no self at all. As you look into a compassionate friend's eye, or catch your reflection in a shop window, you will find yourself beside yourself, loving and lovable, capable of creating any change you need.

Bitter Irony

The way to be happy is to be comfortable with being unhappy. The way to gain knowledge is to be comfortable with not knowing. The way to become comfortable is leave our comfort zone. It's no wonder we get confused and lose ourselves.

The direct route to happiness is the indirect route. Our most natural habit is to pursue happiness. We see something that we think will make us happy and we run after it. Happiness loves that game. It just runs and runs ahead of us. When we stop chasing happiness and immerse ourselves in what we are doing, happiness tends to stop running and come to us.

Although following your desires will bring you happiness, fulfilling your desires will not. Desire itself is a form of pain. The most obvious way to release the pain is to satisfy the desire. The less obvious way is going after the desire rather than the object of the desire. Observing the pain of the want, the discomfort, will lead to an understanding of yourself. Understanding your Self will lead to happiness.

Sadness, boredom, discomfort, wanting, and not knowing are all good places to begin the practice of understanding yourself. That practice will invite happiness. When you understand that you don't understand yourself, you will begin to understand your Self. Your Self bubbles over with a delightfully bitter joy.

The Unknown

There is a lot to fear in the unknown. There is also a lot of comfort to be found in the unknown. If you knew that you would die at the end of the week, you would likely spend your week differently than you would living as you do in the unknown. Society values knowledge and shuns ignorance. Because of these values, many of us spend our lives pretending we know all sorts of things that we don't. We like to be seen as knowledgeable. We don't like to be thought of as ignorant. This way of thinking is ignorance and we should know that.

Everyday, children, youth and adults rush off to school and work to tackle the unknown. We gather information, facts and experiences from the vast world of the unknown and collect them in our tiny world of the known. Some things we all know and we consider that to be common knowledge. In each section of society and in each culture there is a shared understanding that should be known by everybody. In the city, common knowledge is knowing to cross the street when the light is green, in the jungle it is knowing which snakes are poisonous. In the jungle, it is fine to be ignorant of traffic laws and in the city, there are more pressing poisons to understand. Yet, when we encounter a person who is lacking in common knowledge, we imagine that person to be stupid or ignorant. When we imagine that kind of thing about others we also imagine it about ourselves. We fear that we too, may be stupid or ignorant. That is the fear of the unknown.

When we understand that knowledge is relative and contextual, we don't have to worry about being stupid and ignorant. All human knowledge amounts to a grain of sand on the beach of the unknown. When we embrace our ignorance, we can drop the pretense of appearing to have special knowledge. We can then focus on exploring the unknown and using what we find to help each other get along in life. Who knows what we can accomplish?

Why You Matter

People experience a lot of stress from imagining that they don't matter. If you didn't matter, you would not stress over whether you matter or not. You matter because you suffer. Before you suffered, you didn't even concern yourself with whether you mattered or not. You knew you mattered. When you got hungry, you knew you needed food. When you got tired you needed sleep. As a baby you understood that you mattered so much that you cried out to let the world know whenever you needed something.

Now, when you feel heavy with all there is to do and what you are supposed to be, you start to wonder about what the point is to all that suffering. All that suffering is there to show you how much you matter. Each time you suffer, you feel for yourself. You feel a connection to the world. You want the suffering to stop because it matters to you that you feel good. It matters when you don't.

When you can see significance in your suffering, you see the heart of compassion. You can connect with any other human or animal that suffers. You know that you all matter immensely. That brings you comfort and your suffering passes.

When you learn how to stop suffering, then you still matter because you can help others who suffer. They may not know that they matter, but you know, so you can set them straight.

As You Are

You are entirely lovable as you are. People who feel unlovable underestimate both the capacity of love and themselves. These kinds of miscalculations can lead to misery. Also, misery can lead to these kinds of miscalculations. If you feel unlovable, you will feel miserable. If you feel miserable, you may feel unlovable. Many people are miserable. Nobody is unlovable.

As you contemplate love, you are absolutely lovable. If you imagine somebody suffering because they feel unlovable, then your heart goes out to them. You immediately send love their way. Yet even though you can contemplate love and feel love, you can still imagine that there is something about you that is unlovable.

As you are, right now, people love you. That love may not be the love you want, or demonstrated the way you need, but just as you are, you are loved. Love is huge. Nobody is immune.

Self-Harm, Eating Disorders, Control, and the Buddha

Buddha's path to end his suffering brought him through an ascetic period where he restricted his diet to the brink of starvation and endured self-inflicted pain to his body. When he experienced enlightenment, he realized that the path to end suffering did not need to follow these practices.

Buddha's experience was different from that of people who practice self-harm and suffer from eating disorders, but the suffering that he was addressing was the same. He was in a desperate search for control. His control was supposedly over the cycle of life and death. For people of different cultures, who are more concerned with this life than the next, that control is not so much control of anything, but a struggle for a sense of control. The struggle for this sense of control can lead to a total loss of control and unimaginable suffering.

Buddha experienced a full recovery when he realized that there was nothing controlling and nothing to control. The cycle of life and death continued without him. He returned to eating normally and he stopped creating painful circumstances for his body. He was filled with compassion for those who continued to suffer.

Like Buddha, people who suffer from eating disorders and self-harm are incredibly aware. They experience peace in the midst of extreme suffering. From a Buddhist perspective, we are all buddhas, and can all awaken to a Self that is beyond harm. That keen awareness, inquiring into the question of what is controlling what, can help separate the peace from the suffering. When the suffering is gone, the peace will remain. The wisdom acquired when we learn to transform suffering into peace can be used to help others along the path.

Dealing With Your Mother

There is a powerful mindfulness practice called Dealing with Your Mother. This is an especially important practice for those still living in the same house as their mothers. This practice is helpful for anybody at any age. When you have mastered this practice, you will be able to deal with everything else.

Our mothers have an important place in our lives. They can inspire intense love or intense hate and all the intense emotions in between. They are closely aligned with our egos because they were there when our egos were created. Intentionally and unintentionally, consciously and unconsciously, they can push all of our buttons. When our mothers are not around, we find other people to push those buttons, but nobody can do it quite like mom.

To practice dealing with your mother you have to pay special attention to your interactions with your mother and the emotions evoked in those interactions. Practice looking at the situation through your mother's eyes. If your most basic assumption is that you love your mother, use that love to power your practice. If your mother suffers, connect with her suffering. When you see past your own suffering to the suffering of somebody that you love, you gain strength and courage.

It is helpful in Dealing with Your Mother to address the surface issues. After an incident occurs, talk to your friends and develop a strategy for the next time something like that happens. If you are prone to angry exchanges with your mother, focus on trying to stay with your anger without getting carried away by it. If you get carried away despite your strategy, wipe the slate clean and try again the next time. Your mother will still be there.

Moonlighting

You have two jobs in life. The first is to do everything that you need to do. The second is to be who you need to be, so that you do not suffer through doing your first job.

The first job is not the first job because it is more important. The first job is first because that's what you did first in life. Before you got your first job, you had no job. You just did whatever it was that you did with your time. Once you got into school and started taking on responsibilities, then you had your first job. You acquired all sorts of things that you needed to do. Along with acquiring all those things to do, you acquired all sorts of things that you needed to be. Being just what you needed to be to do what you needed to do became your second job. The second job is no more or less important than the first. You can do neither job without the other.

Working two full time jobs can wear you down, so naturally, you begin to suffer. Unfortunately, you have no choice but to do these jobs. To be who you are, you have to do what you need to do. To do what you need to do, you have to be who you are. If doing what you need to do and being who you are is causing you too much suffering, then you have to make changes.

You are not what you do. If you are working at being who you are, then that is not who you are. You can quit that job. You can just be yourself. That is enough. When you can effortlessly be who you are, then it becomes much easier to do what you need to do. What you do no longer impacts who you are. Who you are is no longer dependent on what you do. As long as you are, you will do. Enjoy the moonlight.

Ego Games

Egos love to play games. They make up all sorts of rules for their games and we just follow those rules. One of ego's favorite games is *Successful Self*. It creates an image of success in our mind and we have to bend over backwards to become that successful person.

The tricky part about becoming a successful person is that the criteria for success constantly changes. Success could be being happy, being smart, being rich, or famous. Success can measured in the distant future, near future, past or present.

As long as we play the ego's game of *Successful Self*, we will experience the self-esteem highs and lows that come with that game. Sometimes we will be winning and seem quite successful. Other times we will be losing and will notice all the success vanish, exposing us as complete failures. We can be wildly successful in a thousand different ways, but one imagined failure could throw the whole match.

The only way to win a game of *Successful Self* with your ego is to recognize the game. When you see the game and the ego and all the amazing and ridiculous things you have done to appear successful, you will notice that your True Self is an unqualified success. It has succeeded in winning and losing, and feeling, and loving, and even coming to recognize itself. Once you notice the ego's game, you can continue to play it. You are playing with house money though. You can try to make yourself believe that you are not so successful so that the game seems authentic, but you will know that despite all the ups and downs you go through, the game is just measuring mountains with teaspoons. Success and failure are just games egos play.

Ego Improv

There is a custom in improvisational theater that when an actor suggests a scenario, the other actors go with it. They just say yes to whatever comes along. If you're doing improv and your partner asks, "Is your head stuck in the banister again?", you would say, "It's my third time today, I can't believe my luck". That saying yes prevents arguments on stage and creates comedy. That same trick can be used in everyday life to challenge your ego.

It's so easy to get stuck worrying what other people think of you. Your ego wants others to see you just as you want to be seen. If they think something about you that isn't true, you may get embarrassed or angry because they have the wrong idea about you. If you notice this happening, you can just use the improv trick and pretend to be what the people think of you. You don't have make a comedy routine of your life, but you can do it in your mind. Pretend, just for a moment, that you are what others think you are. Don't fight it, but pretend it, knowing that it's not true.

When you feel hurt by what somebody thinks of you and you react with anger or embarrassment, then you are believing their misconception. When you pretend to be what they think you are, then you can easily see that they are wrong and their mistaken opinion won't hurt you so much. Each time you try this trick, your ego will shrink a little. Your True Self, which is impervious to judgement, will shine through. You're a star.

Excuse Me

You don't need an excuse to be who you are. That is who you are. When you suffer from guilt, it always seems like there is something wrong that needs to be excused. It could be something you've done, or something you haven't done. It could be something you did on purpose or it could be something you did by accident. It could be something that somebody else did. It could be nothing at all. For all that, you are excused.

You pile yourself with expectations and other people pile their own expectations on you. Sometimes these expectations are contradictory, so by meeting one expectation you fall short of another. It is impossible to meet all those expectations. You are excused for not accomplishing the impossible.

If you suffer from guilt because you have actually done something wrong, then you are lucky, because you can apologize or try to correct what you have done. If don't know why, but you feel guilty anyway, then you need a general excusing. You are just fine as you are, trying your best to be happy under difficult circumstances. For that, you are fully and completely excused. Carry on.

I Beg Your Pardon

The monks back in Buddha's time were called beggars. That was their practice and their sustenance. Each day the beggars and the Buddha would go into the towns and beg for their daily meal. They were well respected as they begged. They didn't beg for money because they could not eat money. They begged for food and they shared whatever they received with the community, because some got more and some got less and some were not able to make their begging rounds.

In our capitalist societies, we don't like beggars. We believe that what's mine is mine and what's yours is yours. If you want what I have, you should work hard for it and then you will both have what I have and appreciate it more because you worked for it. That's not really true.

We are all beggars. Some of us are just better at begging than others and we are able to get more. Then we forget to share with those that are less able to beg than we are. Besides not sharing what we received through our particular style of begging, we justify not sharing by imagining that others are less deserving than us. This not sharing and looking down on people makes us uncomfortable. It's even worse if we are in need and nobody is sharing with us. Then we may feel like people are looking down on us and we feel unworthy of receiving what they have. Whether we have, or have not, because we are beggars and don't like beggars, we come into conflict with ourselves.

As we all beg our way through life, it is helpful to like beggars. It is wonderful to both give and receive help from those around us. Sharing, being generous, and being gracious nourishes happiness. Disliking beggars, nourishes contempt. We are all deserving of our daily meal. We are all beggars. We are all Buddha.

Becoming Buddhist

We all have these amazing egos that like nothing more than to accessorize life. Just like getting a new, expressive case for our new phone, the ego tries to make the self more solid by dressing it up with all kinds of characteristics. We are born into certain characteristics and we choose others. We are each born into a family and we have a body with a race and a culture, which often includes a religion. We are each given a name and we learn to associate all of those characteristics into our sense of who and what we are, our self.

We tend to strongly identify with those characteristics, which we think are permanent, such as our facial features, our ethnicity, our gender, or our race. Religion is one of the characteristics that sits near what we think of as the core of our being. In society, all of these various roles come with behavioral expectations. We start to suffer when we notice that these core identities and associated expectations are in conflict with our experience. When we suffer, we start scrambling to change ourselves and associate new characteristics with our sense of self. When we begin the task of aligning ourselves toward a more comfortable truth, we often look to a new religion. It seems that we can become a whole new person when we toss out one set of expectations and take on another.

Buddhism is a great religion for people seeking happiness, but there is no need to become a Buddhist. Buddha wasn't a Buddhist, he was just Buddha. He was a Hindu and a prince and intensely uncomfortable with the expectations associated with his identity. As you seek a new identity, you start right where you are, with your present identity and associated expectations and suffering. You are just like Buddha. If you follow the path of Buddhism, you eventually learn that you are Buddha. There is no need to become a Buddhist as you explore your identity. You only need to be Buddha, which you are.

Life and Death

All we know is life. We don't know anything about death. We know what life is like when somebody else dies, but that's all we know about death. We know that one day we will die. Even our own death is an abstract concept. We know nothing about death.

We think about death as a loss. When somebody dies we say we lost that person. We put them in the ground and mark the site with a stone so that we can always find them. We grieve because we lost a loved one. Grieving is necessary to process the feelings associated with the life changes that death brings. Death is not necessarily a loss. We don't know, we only know life.

Although unknowable, death is a part of life. Our lives have the quality of being, with the certain potential of someday not being. We are fine with the not being that was us before we were born. We survived that. The prospect of not being again, after life, is more unsettling. We have more important things to worry about though. We worry about what we know, life.

When we worry our way through life, it is helpful to think about death. To know death in life, we can practice seeing death in each change of circumstance. Who you were yesterday is gone.

Who you will be tomorrow is as unknowable as death. Tomorrow you will get to know life again.

Part 4

Sweet Liberation

World Peace

There are short-term and long-term effects of meditation. In the short-term, after just a few minutes of meditation, we may feel some peace. The long-term effect of meditation is world peace. The long-term is very long term. People have been meditating since people have been people and world peace has not quite happened yet. The moon is at peace. The stars are at peace, even the earth is at peace, but, on the surface, there continues to be widespread suffering. That is why we need to keep meditating.

If everybody in the world were busy meditating, we would not have time to shoot each other. Also, after all that meditation, we would have no inclination to shoot each other. Meditation gives people a sense of connectedness, which interferes with the impulse to hurt each other. On a personal level, that sense of connectedness also interferes with the impulse to hurt ourselves. When we sit in meditation we are connected to the earth beneath our cushion and the moon and the stars above. When we get up, we are still connected, but we are often more distracted and we might forget about peace.

In our busy lives, it's hard to know what we can do to create world peace. We feel small and insignificant in the face of global forces. We may even feel ineffectual in dealing with our own minds. Those feelings are an indication that we could use some peace. When that happens, we have to sit on our cushion, or sofa, or subway seat, or in our stealth bomber cockpit, or on our aircraft carrier, in our square or oval office, and breathe deeply, feel the peace above and below us, then share that peace with each other. Meditation takes only a few minutes a day. It can change the world.

Basically Good

To let go of your worries and allow things to just be, it helps to believe that things are basically good. You shouldn't assume such a radical belief without gathering evidence. The evidence for basic goodness is all around you. When you look at flowers, stars, kittens, candles, cuddles, you see signs of the goodness in the world. The foods that you normally eat are delicious to you. When you're thirsty, nothing tastes better than water. The fact that we perceive beauty in so many naturally occurring phenomena is evidence that there is basic goodness in the world.

Yet, amid all this goodness there is great suffering. There are people who intentionally harm others, or are indifferent to the suffering that they cause. This may seem like evidence of a basic evil in the world, which challenges the idea of basic goodness. The fact that a volcano, earthquake or asteroid can wipe out a city or civilization, may seem like evidence of basic indifference.

Good, evil and indifference are all certainly present in the world. If you hate everything and live to create suffering, then you believe in basic evil. If you don't care about anything, then you believe in basic indifference. If you want to enjoy life and help others enjoy life, then you believe in basic goodness. When you recognize the basic goodness in the world, you can harmonize with goodness wherever you find it.

When you recognize basic goodness, you are prepared to handle all of life's circumstances.

So Logically...

Buddha tried all kinds of spiritual tricks before he experienced enlightenment. Once he experienced what he experienced he knew that the experience was possible for everybody, so he set about trying to teach everybody how to have that experience. That was 2500 years ago. In human time, we are slow learners.

Now that Buddha experience, that dawning of awareness, that opening of the mind's eye, that suffering to end all suffering, that awakening was accomplished by just sitting there, watching, not knowing what to expect. However, once he experienced that, he knew that he knew what he knew. He knew that he had something to teach. He knew that his experience could not be passed through logic alone. It was beyond logic.

However, because Buddha was able to see this and teach the way beyond logic for others to see it, and because others have seen it, in all kinds of spiritual and intellectual endeavors, that demonstrates that it is there to be seen. Spiritual seekers, philosophers, random awakeners, have seen it in the East, West, North and South. It is one of the experiences that is common and available to everybody.

To use logic to go beyond logic is tricky. However, logic can still point the way. If there is a way to end all of your suffering simply by changing how you think, then logic will tell you that suffering is a matter of thinking. You are already essentially enlightened, just like the Buddha. What do you think about that?

Once and for All

Imagine experiencing a purely psychological phenomenon, which would improve your outlook forever. Imagine that you could experience a particular awareness that would change how you understand the nature of existence and fill you with a sense of peace, joy and love.

Now, imagine that this experience is not just an experience that you can experience like you can experience a movie. If a certain movie is playing in a certain movie theater, you can experience that movie by going there and buying a ticket. Imagine that this experience can only be experienced by believing in it, sight unseen, and then looking for it in each and every experience that you have.

Once you believe that this experience exists and could possibly happen at anytime as you pay attention to your immediate senses of taste, touch, smell, sight, sound or thought, then those constant experiences begin to improve your outlook. Your understanding of the nature of existence changes and you begin filling with a sense of peace, joy and love.

Healing the Past

If something hurt you ten years ago or ten minutes ago, you have now suffered long enough from that pain. That past suffering was inevitable. You have lived through it and learned from it. It has shaped who you are, but it is no longer essential to who you are becoming. Now is the time to let that hurt heal.

The way to let that hurt heal is not to forget it and move on. That is impossible. We remember everything. The way to let it heal is to immerse yourself in the present, where that particular pain is a memory. You can breathe in a deep healing breath and feel the longstanding, familiar pain for a farewell visit. Then breathe out again. If you are still there, then you have survived. You can try it again if necessary.

Who you are does not rely on the pain of the past. You can live without it, especially if it is difficult to live with it. Who you are in the present is somebody who has survived and now has a completely different set of circumstances in your life. As you continue into the future, you can meet past and present pain with the same resolve and heal it upon first contact. That can save you a lot of carrying. Although you have proven that you are strong enough to carry all that pain, you don't need to anymore. You can now use those emotional muscles to carry peace. You deserve peace.

The Present

Giving and getting presents is a way to happiness. The giving is a great way to be generous. The getting is a great way to be grateful. The exchange is about love. It's not at all about the present. The present is a token of love, generosity and gratitude. If it were only about the present, we might overlook the love and generosity that went into it. We might miss out on the gratitude, if we become too focused on an object, which might, or might not, bring us happiness.

The gift-wrapped present is a good analogy for our search for our True Nature. We look at ourselves and we see a wrapped gift. We are here because of the generosity and love of others and for that we can feel gratitude. When we look at ourselves as a wrapped present, we can see all the potential of greatness within us. Beneath the wrapping lies the potential for unbounded happiness.

Imagine we are given such a gift and told what is inside. We can't wait to unwrap it, so we tear into it. Then we find another wrapped box. For a while that is amusing, but as we keep unwrapping layer after layer, we lose sight of the generosity and love that created the present and we become too busy trying to get at that happiness inside to feel gratitude.

We get so caught up in ripping through the layers of wrapping that we miss how carefully and beautifully each layer is wrapped. Getting to the center becomes a tedious chore. Because we know that the gift contains unlimited happiness, we slog on, layer after layer, hoping that the next layer will be the last. Even though we would like to get through all that wrapping, we have other things to do with our lives than unwrap an impossibly concealed treasure.

Fortunately, we got the gift down to a size that we can put it in our pocket and work at it in the few spare moments in our busy schedules and in the middle of the night when we can't sleep.

Carrying that gift around, however, begins to affect our lives. With unlimited happiness in our pocket, we don't get so concerned with the ups and downs of our busy lives. Whenever we get overwhelmed and lose touch with love and generosity and gratitude, we can sit down and unwrap a few more layers of our present. That brings us great peace.

Whether or not we ever get to the unlimited happiness at the heart of our gift, depends on how we approach it. When trying to get to the center of the present has filled us to overflowing with gratitude, love and generosity, then naturally, we will give our gift away.

Pretending

Everyday day we pretend. We play a giant game of make-believe. We are all children role-playing our lives. We are exceptionally good pretenders. We are so good that we don't even know we are pretending.

When we lie, we know we are pretending. We let our words pretend something is true when we know it is not. Sometimes, when we smile, we are pretending. If we're not feeling happy, but we don't want to burden the world with out troubles, we will pretend to be happy. When we are not happy, it is not because we intend to pretend that we are in a miserable set of circumstances, it is because we actually believe that to be true. We are playing somebody else's game of make believe. We measure ourselves with a make believe yardstick that tells us we are tiny, or huge, or good or bad. We all want to be good, but when we measure ourselves, we pretend that the instrument is real and we feel good or bad depending on our measurements.

We have to believe something. That's what we do. We constantly sort the world into true and false and good and bad and we believe that's how it is. We consciously and unconsciously pretend. We believe and make believe. We believe things that are true and false and we make others believe things that are true and false, both on purpose and by accident. Because we spend so much time pretending, believing, measuring, and feeling, consciously and unconsciously, we might as well consciously pretend in ways that make us feel good. When we end up feeling good, we will begin to believe in what we pretend.

If you don't believe that you are truly good and wonderful, that would be a good place to begin with your pretending. Pretend that you're not pretending. When you see that you are pretending the Truth, you won't have to pretend any more. From then on, your games of make believe will wear real smiles.

Holy Cow

There is no such thing as a non-spiritual experience. What is it that would have such an experience? We like to divide and categorize our lives. This habit makes us imagine that sometimes we have regular experiences and other times we have spiritual experiences. Spiritual experiences tend to feel really good. If we eat delicious food, we say it tastes like heaven. When we are so filled with joy that we can barely contain ourselves, we think that we are having a particularly spiritual experience.

In Zen and various other religions and philosophies there is a great deal of emphasis placed on the awakening experience. This experience is held above all others as a glimpse into the truth of the universe. Of course it is wonderful to glimpse into the truth of the universe. That is what we all do, all day and night, all the time.

You can't be spiritual in Church on Sundays, Synagogue on Saturdays, Mosque on Fridays, or meditation on Mondays, then be less spiritual the rest of the week as you hang out with friends or go to school or work. Your most delightful and insightful experiences are no more spiritual than your shallowest indulgences.

If you feel like there is some sort of spiritual value in the world, then that is your world, day and night, in sickness and in health. You are that essence. The most spiritual moments are not marked by blazing lights and blaring trumpets, they are every single moment that there is. There is light everywhere and equal holiness in darkness. You can sing in the church choir, chant in the Zendo or yodel in the shower. It's all one spiritual moment after the next. Holy cow.

Windowing

Trying to help people is a tricky business. Some of the best intentioned people looking to help others come raging into a situation with their helping agenda and end up making the situation worse. If you have a truck to help your friend move, that can be helpful. If your friend doesn't want to move, loading your truck with their belongings is just burglary. This can happen even with self-help. Sometimes the best way to help is to do nothing. Help like a window helps.

A window is nothing. It is a hole in the wall. Yet the light shines through that hole and brings light to the room. This is how meditation works. You sit, doing nothing, and the light shines through you. Your attention is light. When you allow your attention to rest on your thoughts and the feelings that feed on those thoughts, the thoughts will be transformed. When you become a conduit for light, you can help others. You don't have to do anything to help but allow light into the situation. Put your attention on their problems and let the light do its thing.

If you see a homeless person on the street, you don't have to give change. You can, but you can also be a window, illuminating the world wherever you go. Change will come.

Eyesight Insight

Eyesight is how we see with our eyes. Insight is how we see with our minds. Both of these abilities are equally amazing. Our eyes, don't care what they see. They see whatever they are pointed toward. They take in all the light available to them and the report that to the mind. The mind then decides what to do with that light and where to point the eyes.

Eyes can see beauty and ugliness equally. The mind prefers beauty. When the eyes see ugliness, the mind may shut them, or point them in another direction. The eyes don't mind though. They are not happy to be rid of the ugliness or sorry to be plunged into darkness. That is the burden of the mind.

With all the incredible things that our eyes see, we forget how amazing it is that we can see. With the incredible things that our minds can do, we can still get insight from our eyesight.

All Your Fault

If you feel like everything is your fault, you can find liberation in that feeling. Imagine that everything is actually your fault. You caused the sun to shine and the wind to blow. You created a world full of joy and suffering and you chose to get right down in the mud and suffer along with your creation.

If everything is your fault, you don't have to waste any more of your energy finding fault or assigning blame. You've magnanimously taken that responsibility on yourself. There is no need to get angry at others because they can't help themselves. They only do as you please. Please.

If you are suffering and think that you somehow deserve to suffer for what others do or did, then you need a way to expel that idea from your mind. One way to get rid of that idea is to look right at it and see it for what it is. You don't even need forgiveness when there is nothing to forgive. That is freedom.

Strength of Surrender

When we are faced with difficult emotions, we sometimes try to be strong and contain ourselves. We believe that it is weak to let our emotions out and strong to keep them in. We may feel that way with sadness. With anger, it is the opposite. When we let our anger out we may feel or or think we're strong, even if we are raging lunatics.

The release of anger can be the result of trying to hold in sadness or hurt. If we have the strength to feel our sadness and our hurt, that is true strength. That kind of strength can allow our feelings to pass without causing additional problems like worrying that we are weak or falling into rages.

Strength is dealing with the world as it is and finding peace, love and compassion despite difficult circumstances. It takes amazing strength to surrender your armor and expose your tender heart to the world. That kind of strength will bring you freedom.

Humility

The way to transcend humiliation is with humility. A truly humble person cannot be humiliated. They don't even feel humility. Practicing humility, like any mindfulness practice is easier when you are not suffering. If you are cruising along, feeling good about life, it is easy to appreciate life and not think much about yourself. If life is knocking you down and it feels like one humiliating experience after another, you feel terrible and think about yourself a lot. That terrible feeling of, *I'm not good enough,* can ring like a bell, to remind you to practice humility.

A bright side to not feeling good enough is that you are not falling for the deception that you are better than others. Unfortunately, you are falling for the deception that others are better than you. Humility is understanding that you are simply existing and ideas that you are good or bad are extra. Transforming humiliation into humility is humbly heroic. However, when you make that transformation, humility leaves you feeling more humble than heroic.

When you are truly humble you are not concerned with humility or humiliation. If you notice yourself feeling humiliation, let that feeling ring like a bell, reminding you to practice humility. Bow, and honor all that is good in you and the world. Ding.

Zen Cow

What does a Zen cow say?
Mu. Moooooooooooooooo.

In Zen circles, there is a famous koan about
mu. Mu is Chinese for Nothingness or no. When a
disciple asked the master Joshu if a dog has a
Buddha Nature, Joshu said 'Mu'. This was a
confounding answer, because every Buddhist
understands that everything has a Buddha Nature,
including dogs. The answer was intended to
awaken the disciple to his own Buddha Nature.
That story has been used since that time to awaken
countless seekers to their own Buddha Natures.
Today certain Zen practitioners will sit in
meditation and contemplate mu until they awaken.
Mu, mu, mu, mu, mu. They try not to think about
anything else while they think about nothing. Just
like a cow.

The joke of this joke is Zen. There is no such
thing as a Zen cow. Cows are just cows. They say
moo. People are also just people. As people, we
suffer. We suffer from our thoughts. We think we
are things that we are not. We think we are good
cows, or bad cows, or Christian cows, or Buddhist
cows, or Muslim cows, or Hindu cows, or Jewish
cows, or atheist cows, or black cows or white cows,

or milk cows or beef cows. We're not even cows. Mu.

Liberation of Liberation

The idea that we could be liberated is a liberating idea. The concept that we are already liberated is also liberating. Thinking about liberation, may on the other hand make us feel trapped. In that case, may need to be liberated from the idea of liberation. Whether or not we are liberated by these thoughts depends on what we think of ourselves and of liberation. Liberation, here, now, is freedom from suffering.

If we believe that liberation is possible, that gives us hope. Hope eases our suffering and we are instantly liberated. In that way, the idea that we could be liberated liberates us. In a less immediate sense, the idea that it is possible not to suffer can give us the courage we need to engage with our suffering and find a way through it.

That we may already be liberated is difficult to comprehend when we are suffering. That idea challenges what it is in us that suffers. If we are suffering, but liberated, it's like watching a sad movie. We feel for the characters in the movie and we cry as they go through their movie dramas. We are suffering, but not suffering. Because we went to the movie in order to suffer that way, we feel great as we feel terrible for the movie characters. It is possible that there is a part of us that is completely liberated and moved but unmoved by the suffering in our own lives. That is how we can be free from suffering even as we suffer. That is a way to imagine being free, even as we suffer.

Being liberated from liberation is freely accepting our suffering. That way, when we suffer, we don't even need to be anywhere else but in the midst of our suffering. There is no separation between suffering and not suffering. We are free from the idea that there may be some other way to be.

Being liberated by liberation is how the entity of liberation, entices us to find it. It is there calling to us, encouraging us, as we move in and out of suffering. Finding liberation causes us to seek it. It's backwards, but that's how it works. Liberation liberates us, the liberated, liberating, liberators. Find and ye shall seek. Ha.

The Way (Two Koans)

Joshu asked his Master Nansen, "What is the Way?" Nansen replied, "Ordinary mind is the Way."

Ordinary mind is Buddha Mind. That is good news for everybody with an ordinary mind, which is all of us.

A monk and Zen Master were walking along a mountain stream. The monk asked "How do I enter the Way?" The Master replied, "Do you hear that bubbling stream? Enter there."

You don't need to go to ancient China and find that stream to enter the Way. You don't need any special mind to enter the Way. You just need to use the mind you have and whatever you happen to be experiencing to enter the Way. You might wonder what is so special about the Way if it is just your ordinary mind and ordinary sensations. The Way is special because it is beyond suffering. The fact that it can be accessed through any ordinary experience with an ordinary mind is extraordinary.

Do you feel that suffering? Enter through there. Suffering is an added layer of experience caused by your thinking, opinions, beliefs and judgements. These thoughts are the bubbling mountain stream. If you ever notice yourself suffering, you can notice what you are thinking. Notice what your ordinary mind is doing and enter.

Enter the Way with what you have, where you are.
See where the suffering goes.

The Spirit of Zen

Although Zen is a spiritual tradition, there is nothing spiritual about Zen. There is no specific god in Zen. Buddha was a man, who found a way to live with his mind in such a way that he didn't suffer. He then set about teaching others how to live with their minds. Living with your mind may include worshiping a god or making offerings to the dead. It may include passing from one life to the next. It may not.

The spirit of Zen is the spirit of life. It is nothing more than all of existence and nothing less. If you bow to a statue of the Buddha in your practice, it is not because Buddha is a god and you are something less, it is because you are bowing. If you sit in meditation, you are not any closer to the spirit of the universe than when you sit on the toilet. Both of those activities are part of life.

In god-fearing cultures, it is hard not to imagine a conscious power pulling strings to make things happen. Even atheists may find themselves asking the cosmos for favors in a pinch. Whether God exists or not is beyond the scope of Zen. Not knowing is the spirit of Zen. What is God? What is Buddha? What am I? Don't know. That's the spirit.

Instant and Gradual Enlightenment

Everybody wants instant enlightenment. That is the one that comes with a fireworks show and a few months of elation. Gradual enlightenment is living in suffering until the point of suffering is lost. Either way, everybody is as enlightened as they will be when they realize that they are enlightened. If enlightenment occurs to you through a gradual build up of logic, through hours of focused meditation, or from hearing a stone strike a stalk of bamboo, it is the same enlightenment. It is the same enlightenment that is happening in the midst of your ordinary, everyday life.

One sign of enlightenment is not noticing that you are enlightened. If you don't think that you are enlightened, how can you be sure that you are not? Enlightenment is nothing to strive for, nothing at all.

Changing Your Life

If you've decided that your life needs a change, but you don't know how to go about creating that change, then you might try meditation. If your life feels stagnant and unchanging, or if it feels like it is changing too quickly, meditation works for that. Meditation does not transform your world overnight, but it can give you little pockets of peace, everyday, from which positive changes can grow.

Meditation is a lot like watching television or sitting at the computer, only there is no television or computer. You don't need any special skill, spiritual incline, or religious beliefs. You need to take a few minutes everyday to devote yourself to inviting positive change.

To meditate, find a quiet space where you will not be interrupted. Put a few cushions on a carpeted floor, or sit on a firm chair. Breathe in deeply and breathe out slowly. Do that three of four times, then begin counting your breaths from one to ten.

When your thoughts carry you away from your breaths, return to your breath and start counting again at one.

Keep your eyes open, lightly focused and looking downward to an area about three feet in front of you. Place your hands in your lap. Rest your tongue on the front of the roof of your mouth. Breathe in through your nose and out through your mouth. Try not to squirm. If the sky opens up in front of you, return to your breath, and start counting again at one. Try meditating twice a day for 15-20 minutes at a time.

If this way doesn't work for you, try your own way. Your life will change.

About the Author

On December 28, 2013, at the Awakened Meditation Centre in Toronto, Ontario, Canada, Zen master Bub-In, received Dharma transmission from his teacher and Zen master, Venerable Hwasun Yangil Sunim, who belongs to the Jogye Order of Korean Buddhism.

Zen master Bub-In is also known as Peter Taylor. He practiced social work in Toronto for ten years, where he experienced enough suffering to drive him to a serious meditation practice. He is the author of the blog, Zen Mister (zenmister.com). He currently lives in New Jersey with his wife, Lily, and daughter, Abby.

About the Artist

In the same transmission ceremony, Zen master Hye-Chung received Dharma transmission from her teacher, Venerable Hwasun Yangil Sunim.

Zen master Hye-Chung is also known as Rebecca Nie. She is a professional artist based in Palo Alto California (www.rebexart.com).

About Inroads Press

Inroads Press (inroadspress.com) of Langley, WA is dedicated to promoting accessible and practical inroads into our personal capacities for healing and transformation.

Made in the USA
Middletown, DE
12 October 2016